The
WOMEN
of PLUMS

The
WOMEN
of PLUMS

Poems in the Voices of Slave Women

Dolores Kendrick

William Morrow and Company, Inc.
New York

Library of Congress Cataloging-in-Publication Data

Kendrick, Dolores, 1927–
    The women of plums : poems in the voices of slave women / Dolores Kendrick.
        p.   cm.
    ISBN 0-688-08347-1
    1. Women slaves—Poetry.   2. Afro-American women—Poetry.
    3. Slavery—United States—Poetry.   I. Title.
    PS3561.E423W6   1989
    811'.54—dc 19   89-30197
                                                                                    CIP

Printed in the United States of America

First Edition

1 2 3 4 5 6 7 8 9 10

BOOK DESIGN BY JAYE ZIMET

Acknowledgments

Some of these poems are based upon historical situations. The author wishes to acknowledge the following references: *The American Slave: A Composite Autobiography*, edited by George Rawick, Federal Writers' Project interviews with ex-slaves, 19 volumes and supplements (Westport, Conn.: Greenwood Press, 1972); Library of Congress, Records of Federal Writers' Project, Records Department, Group 69, Works Project Administration; *Black Slave Narratives*, edited by John Bayliss (New York: Macmillan, 1970); *Folk Culture on St. Helena Island, South Carolina*, by Guy B. Johnson (Chapel Hill, N.C.: University of North Carolina Press, 1930); *Black Women in White America: A Documentary History*, edited by Gerder Lerner (New York: Vintage Books, 1973).

The author also wishes to graciously thank the following for their help and support in the making of this book: the Library of the Phillips Exeter Academy, Jacquelyn Thomas, Academy Librarian, the American Antiquarian Society of Worcester, Massachusetts, Richard Schubart, Historian, Sam Allen, David Weber, Fred and Susan Morhart, Ed and Ella Kleiner, the Very Reverend Marcian O'Meara, Ella Mangan, Gwendolyn Books, Myra Sklarew, Michael Harper, Elio Gasperetti, Historian, Mother Mary Thomas and the Benedictine Community of Saint Walburga of Boulder, Colorado, and finally, the community of Yaddo, where these poems were first developed during two residencies, and the National Endowment for the Arts for a grant enabling me to complete this work. Very special thanks to my editor, Randy Ladenheim-Gil.

The following poems first appeared in the following publications of Lotus Press, Detroit, Michigan: "Harriet in Mid-Air," *A Milestone Sampler: 15th Anniversary Anthology*, 1988; "Canticle of a Black Lady," *Now Is the Thing to Praise*, 1984. The title, "The Women of Plums," first appeared in *Now Is the Thing to Praise*.

You smile on your disasters. Can it be that you,
someday, will illuminate the darkness of this song?
                —Hecuba Euripides' *The Trojan Women*

Go up green an' come down ripe.

                —Gulla riddle

O soil where my children grew . . .
O children, hear us; it is your mother who calls.
. . . I lean my old body against the earth
and both hands beat the ground . . .
we are taken, dragged away . . .
under the slave's roof . . .
Ash, as the skyward smoke wing
piled, will blot from my sight the house where I lived once
. . . Did you see, did you hear?
. . . The earth shook, risen . . .
O shaking, tremulous limbs
this is the way, Forward
into the slave's life.

—Hecuba Euripides' *The Trojan Women*

Canticle of a Black Lady

dying asks a question: she gives an answer

Done. Every ounce of it. Fly winds to sea-rocks and break
a round of prayer upon their backs.

Turtles, take notice! You may walk with your eyes upright.
Beasts in the forest, part the noon with your cries.
Stretch your bones into the sun, embrace Amen as you eat
        the air.

It is done! Said. Pronounced. Motioned. Spoken.
        Astonished.
The men of oranges have shed their skins and their flesh is
        puffed
upon weeds. The women of plums are sweet and black.
        Their flesh
is moist with tears of joy! Their dreams are skins the color
        of dusk.
Their ripe dreams bitten into leave a sour sweetness in the
        membranes of the mouth.

The children of quince quiver in the womb; their eyes are
        dowries,
their tongues, soft songs.

And the Bride comes forth carrying peacocks upon her
        fingers, bearing roses in her hair. She comes forth
        beyond the wedding-day and speaks
        I will and *Amen.*

For my mother,
Josephine Merriweather Kendrick

and for the women in my family, whose strong
and gracious presence was my inheritance and whose
lineage I celebrate, as I will not see their like again,

and for Rose Lane, at ninety.

I thank these women
for coming, and I thank
the good God who sent them.

The Women of Plums

The
WOMEN
of PLUMS

To Market, to Market

Arthur Mason's Shopping List,
November 6, 1804

One Black Angus
One Yew
two Hogs
one Spinning Wheel
one Dresser Mirror
one nigger wench & child
   (pay no more than $2,000)
twelve Silver Spoons
four Tea Cups
four saucers
six China Plates
one Pewter Tea-pot

Bill to be paid in full to Tydus Wellington,
   sixth of November, eighteen hundred and four.

Ndzeli in Passage

Longing

for myself in the home of myself:
Dear Sister,
   you were so brave
to jump into the waters
   rather than have
that death that I go to.
   You chose
the final death, the blessed homeland:

I am a coward,
   I could not throw myself
      into the sea,

         Not me.

Listen, Sister, there is a crib-cry
      in my shaking voice:
I have just been born
      pushing through the womb of sorrow
   that is a farewell
      to my blood
and all its heirs.

But there is a grief, Sister,
   that now beats upon my fears
   like a drum.

Remember me.
   Dead as you are, do not forget
   this parting.

Are there gratuities of death?
   One day, come and tell me,
   and I will rejoice.

Night passes over.

There are sounds and hissings.
   My heart weeps in the dark,
   I go from one land to another,
   boat to boat, sea to sea,
creature of dust,
   dying in the windbloom.

Oh, Sister! Our home is shattered!
   All I know of it, or will ever know
   is stuffed between the limbs of a Portuguese ship.
   What will I do without you, Odonga?
Somehow I feel my sanity slipping,
   what is memory is sitting beside me in the dark
   (but I believe it is daylight outside,
   a slip of it stole into the boat a short while ago
   and it, too, now is captive).
Why have we come to this? What am I doing here?

Remember the sunset coming through
the dark, in the village, Ndzeli?
Remember eating pomegranates and figs with Odonga
under a tree at noonday?
Remember the strut of the lion?
Remember, Ndzeli, the kiss of your prince, Atezwa,

21

who, too, now is dead, murdered, gone?
Remember his beautiful smile
stolen from you in the dizzy night?

Now the birds sit alone on the naked limbs of the Kola tree,
Now in the bark of the lion is a whisper,
Now the griot* is silent,
Now I must go quietly into the night that brings no moon.

There is a rattle in the boat, a harder one in my breast,
a striking, a pain, a beating drum with a message of doom.

I have wanted to tell you, Sister, about this pain,
 but I couldn't; you were too close to it and to my
  hope.
 Remember me, for now I journey to the strange,
  unbidden
 land where they will call me Zeli, and my dreams
 will hang from trees like rotten fruit.

Oh, the grief, the grief!
Sister, remember me!

Yet, I am beyond the passage of this boat,
 I go on another journey
 while the cold air spins
 and the great sails pipe,
 and when this vessel finds its final harbor,
 I will not be with it. No, indeed.

Not even my aching breath will please the passions
 of these merchants. My body is at its end.
 The sorrow in the heart tells me
 and I so receive it willingly, joyfully.
 Oh, I celebrate these raptures.

---

*An African storyteller who preserves through memory the local and some-
times national mythology and history of a people.

Sister, I choose the tender way: I will be smoke.

Lifting. Risen. Gone. Free.
My litany, and natural to me.

Leah: in Freedom

I run away
        I keep runnin' away
                they won't let me alone
                        they won't let me bear
my misery to the river
                and out
                        over the sky
                                or even
                                    under the trees
in moles' holes
        and wolves' caves
                and blackberry patches
                        with my feet
skiddin' and bleedin'
            on the thorns
                    and then it rains
                            on my run
as quick as my momma's voice
                on the slippery road
                        to freedom.
They catch me
        all the time they catch me
                    and bring me back
and whip me

'till I'm blind and deaf
and dumb,
and put me in the cabin
where the blood soak my back
like scaldin' water
and take me out to the fields
and whip me some more.

Oh! the sky is so big!
Ain't it?

The trees are so tall!
Ain't they?

The river's so wide!
Ain't it?

Don't you hear?
Cain't you hear

all that callin', Leah?
Leah's gotta go!

And I run again
all twenty-three years of me
all white and black of me
all the angels in me
and the wings
growing out of my armpits
flapping against my thighs
makin' me move
when I can't,
when I don't want to,
when my back is so sore
and painful
that every flight
makes my wings stick to my side sometimes
and keep me slow

and earthbound;
                   all my momma in me.
                              So soon they catch me again
and beat me again.
                   That was the last time for that.
                                        I lay here
on the hard floor on my back
                   only place that's soft:
                              guess it's the flesh,
the wounds that do it,
                   guess it's the salt, too.
                                        So much pain
it don't pain no more,
                   only the want of freedom pains,
                                        only the fear
of dyin' before I'm free.
                   Yesterday they took out
                              one of my front teeth
to identify me
                   in case I 'scape again
                              and now when I ain't doin'
the housework
                   they put me in an iron collar.
                                        Three days they gives me
three days I got for my wings
                   to heal
                              but they's bent and dirty
and tattered, need washin'
                   they's not the same
                              don't round themselves right
somehow.
          I can see the roots of trees now,
                              don't see the tops no more.
The mole and me
          we's on our own.
                         These days I go
                              to my mistress' room
sew her clothes and cloaks
                   though the wounds be still breakin'

through my shawl
                    and I be sore.
                              She got lots of holes
                                        under her armpits
of her dresses:
                    that makes me shiver,
                              think of my momma.
Mistress say, 'good mawnin', Leah'
                                        (won't look at me)
and tell me about faith
                    and Jesus.

Peggy in Killing

Traveling

They done found me,
Lord! They done found me again!
I'm dead and they don't know it.
Sometimes I don't either.

Except the Spirit come
creepin' in my body
like hot fire
and I burn and burn
all inside
turn to dust
blow away out over
they heads when they
finds me cryin' in a sack.

I listens
and listens:
I'm travelin' in my bones
and the Spirit swooshes out
before I gets a chance to say
Amen.

Oh, the wind! the sea!
I'm dead on this boat.

Go 'way. Go 'way, nigger! they says,
so I goes. Don't touch me yet!
Got to get home to my mother!
Ain't that what the Lord say
when He rise from the dead?
Goin' home to his mother?

Won't somebody row this boat
out of hell?

Visions

Cain't be no slave forever,
not me! and my children
all pretty and soft
all wet in they skin
moist like the sea air
they be buryin' me in.

Cain't be no slave forever,
make way, Lord, here I come!
Here I am!
This heah boat they put me on
with my children
'cause I tried to escape
from they dark breaths,
they glories, hallelujahs!
they fine houses and sweet fields,
they murders murders murders!
they coffins stenchin' in they smiles,
they *come heah Peggy,*
dress my little one,
then fix her somethin' to eat,

29

maybe some cake and milk,
and mine sittin' on the stairs
in the cold, in the dark,
waitin' to do some waitin' on
waitin' for the milk to sour
and the cake to crumble,
hearin' all this
without a word, a whimper,
eyes freezin' in they dreams,
hungers freezin' in they dark,
takin' they dreams to supper
like candles meltin',
after 'while no more light,
they walkin' softly
makin' sure they seen and not heard
and they dreams screamin'
in they bright, soft eyes.

My soft little ones!
My children!
My John and Mary and Lottie,
brown and golden-black,
listenin' in the dark,
bright in they Black!

But it be a gift, a gift!
Out of they misery
I become blacker than the skin
of a tree in the rain,
and I be rooted
in the rich black earth.
Out of me flies the swallow.

Lord, I'm here 'cause I went:
with my little ones; we're
all goin' to somethin' better.
They has to be somethin' better,
and my death give me a chance.

Capture

Cain't be no slave forever,
No, Lord!
I've got wisdom and hope
and I don't think about it,
don't believe it
don't not believe it
don't carry them around
in my misery
like sick animals.

Gotta let go! Gotta live inside death
in a wheelchair, if I must,
there be some energy left in that!

Caught me in Philadelphia,
put me in a boat
down, down in the hollows
of its ribs, in the hollerin'
of the sea
with my three little ones
cryin' to me:
no, I lies.
They be silent,
no tears, no murmers,
no moans, no sighs.

And I knew then
that death give me a chance,
a great salvation,
a fine, early night.

So I waits.

In the dark and dampness
I sat there 'till my skin broke
and I held my children close.

31

The Killing

But that boat wasn't meant
for nothin' but glory,
and when it crashed into the sea,
I entered that water
like I was being baptized,
saw my John's head
stretch among the waves
and near him Mary
and near her Lottie, laughin'.
Oh, Lord! what a sight!
Baptized to the death!

I denounce you, Satan!
I denounce this unfree callin',
I denounce shackles, bondage,
escape, darkness,
the quiet of the pain
in my throat when I scream
for nothin', nothin' at all,
when I watch my children
sit on stairwells
in the dark
and ice forms
in they mouths,
I denounce the evil of rememberin',
I denounce pieces of property,
pounds of pain.

Nothin' be free, but the misery.

My hands over they heads
was such a little matter,
'jes takin' them under
puttin' them there

for the water to purify
for they own bloomin'
under the sea.

Lottie, she kicked a bit,
but that be all.
It be over.

They be flowers under the water now.
Yes!

Lord, how cleansed I be!
When the water come rushin'
beatin' 'gainst my bosom
through me to them,
I feel like I be givin' suck
and the sea be my milk,
and my healthy babies be fed
and wholesome and warm forever.

The Last Vision

I'm here now
in this place
don't know it
but it moves,
and they be water about:
'nother boat.
I can see a tiny window,
but the light hurts
and wants the dark.
Now and then some peoples
come and look at me,
ask me if I wants to eat,
leave me some cornbread
and cold tea.

They be crates and trunks here,
like the other boat,
and I think we be movin'.
They found me in the water,
I reckon, brought me again
in a backward time.

I'm dead.
I know it 'cause I'm happy.
The children are flowers now,
baptized in joy and hope;
I shiver when I think
of they beauty.
Cain't cry, 'cause I be dead,
this old tarp 'round me,
my flesh rottin', my bones
dryin' out, my eyes movin'
through some kind of cheesecloth,
like a fog.

I'm goin' to reach out now,
soon,
so my death
will stay away from my babies:
cain't upset them now!
They's pure.
And these ghosts that come
and watch me in the night?
I'll sing to them,
like a star.

Sophie, Climbing the Stairs

One / O-N-E

Stair / S-T-A-I-R

Two / T-W-O

Stairs / S-T-A-I-R-S

(gotta remember the *S,* mo' than one!)

This learnin' to count and spell at the same time
be a nuisance, but I've gotta do it. Only way

to learn somethin' in this world. Thank the lawd for
Uncle James. He knows how to read and write and count!

Massa's got nothin' on him!

Five / F-I-V-E

Stairs / S-T-A-I-R-S

Run outta stairs soon, then where will you be, Sophie?
Run outta breath, too, then what use are you, Sophie?

But these stairs be of no use, no use at all, unless
they hep Sophie walk her way up to readin' and writin'.

Uncles James' idea. Good one, too.

Eight / E-I-G-H-T

Strange sound; *eight* with an *E*. Why don't they spell *ate*
with an *E*, too, sound the same, don't make sense. Should
    be
an *A*, but no I heard Massa spell somethin' out to Missus

the other day ('cause he didn't want me to know what he
    was sayin')
and he mentioned *eight* and spelled it with an *E*. I
    remembered
the letters and told Uncle James and he told me *eight*, come
    to

think of it, I remembered all the letters Massa spelled out
and Uncle James told me everything he said. Poor Ole
    Massa
had lost eight dollars that day gamblin' on a dog fight.

He needed to borrow ten more dollars from Missus to pay
    his debts
around the town. Well, he got me free, almost, paid about
    twelve
hundred dollars for me, but I worked that off long ago.

Right now, I'm profit.

Twelve / T-W-E-L-V-E

Finished. At the top. Days gettin' longer and my breath
gettin' shorter, but my memory be still young and askin'.
There be the period and the commas, the stops and the
    shorts,

And the periods put an end to everything and don't let
  you go
no further, don't play 'round with periods, Uncle James
  says,
they the be-all and end-all, don't believe in takin' long
  walks

in the fields when you're tired, don't believe in too much
  moanin'
and misery, just bring things into focus when you least
  'spect
and bring the Lawd's truth up to your doorsill, if you can.

No, don't fool 'round with them periods. Got lots of them
  in my
pocket. Savin' them for my children when they ole' enough
  to spend them.

But the comma, gotta learn that better. Say my prayers
  with a period.
Listen to Missus with a comma.

Twelve tribes of Israel
sittin' in a tree,

Daniel in the Lion's mouth,
Lawd, deliver me!

Take this hot milk to Missus' room and see if the two of
  them
start spelling' things out again that they don't want me to
  know.

Wants to know the baptism of words.

The Ballad of Bethany Veney

We were lovers bread and bone
forlorn and full of hope,
and we had dreams,
yes, plump, rich dreams:
escape and then elope,

Oh, yes, escape and then elope!

John and me through cave and field
would take our bodies free
and leave the land,
its MasterMan:
no more his property.

No Lord! No more his property!

The Master, he be quick behind,
for John he be too late,
and me at the appointed place
that we agreed to wait,

to wait. Oh Glory! Just to wait.

And when old Kibber came upon
us running brave and free,
he made John climb
(for the last time)
the way away from me,

　　　　　　　Good God! the way away from me.

I screamed and kicked
and screamed again,
Oh, never did I die
as many times as on that night
my Johnny said Goodbye.

　　　　　　　Sweet Lord! My Johnny said Goodbye.

Don't fight, he whispered on my breast,
and took my hand so cold,
he quivered then
and put an end
to what is bought and sold,

　　　　　　　Oh, yes, to what is bought and sold.

Old Kibber whipped him to the horse
that Johnny rode that night,
I leaped and grabbed his hand again
and kissed away that sight,

　　　　　　　that sight! that killing, suffering sight!

Oh, Betty, 'tis no use, he said,
and Kibber called to me:
go get his clothes,
beware of those
who think they can be free,

　　　　　　　from me! who think they can be free!

39

Oh, never! Never! will I give
my Johnny's clothes to you!
Oh, evil man! Oh, devil man!
your death be surely due!

> *Yes, Lord! Your death be surely due!*

And Johnny said, It 'tis no use,
his face was wet and sore,
I touched his cheek,
Oh, John don't speak,
don't leave me anymore.

> *Sweet John, don't leave me anymore.*

Forgive me, friend, Oh, Johnny John!
I can't go 'way from you.

My Betty, love,
by God above
do what you best must do!

> *Brave girl! Do what you best must do!*

I went and got my Johnny's things
and put them in a sack,
and knew as sure as my heart jumped
he wasn't coming back.

> *No, Lord. He wasn't coming back.*

I've given you some things to eat,
some lamb, a little cake,
the Lord's good book,
the ring I took
to keep your heart awake!

> *Alive! to keep your heart awake.*

My anger, too, I swallowed soft
so he could go in peace,
and held his hand in mine until
my weeping all did cease,

for John! My weeping all did cease.

There are no tears in me tonight
as I sit by the fire
and dream of John
forever gone
my life and lost desire.

Yes, God! my life and lost desire.

Sweet Jesus! in that silvery night,
I heard a small bird sing,
her throat was mine, her feathers mine,
my John was in her wing.

Sweet Lord! my John was in her wing.

Prunella's Picnic

She chats . . .

Day takes off my skin:
wonder where my kin
be today?

You know, Tula?

Here, eat this poke
an' bread

Nothin' dead
today

Tula. Jes' you
an' me in the
kitchen

eatin' these leftovers
'fo they spoil.

Ain't said
much, Tula.

What you think?

with Tula

Day be dead,
Prunella,

too much of it
gone

ahead of me.

Cain't catch up
with it.

Poke good,
yo' bread
nice an' hot.
Always the best.

Even the water
be good.
Gotta git me
some rest.

Gettin' old.

Your kin be sold
lak all of us,
Prue

one time
or 'nother
we all be sold.

My brother be
in Georgia,

I believe.

No mother
I can remember.

Brought somethin'
fo' you,
Heah.

She drinks from a white bowl

Milk.
sun be eighty year
good today,
Tula.
Shines hard,
don't it?
This heah milk
be good from yo' hands,
creamy an' warm,
ripe from the cow's belly.

Why you weep?

She eats an orange

Stole this one.
Sweet.
Look heah, Tula,
take half.
Eat.
Why you weep?

Oranges be
my dessert
every day.
Steal one
every day:
good fo'
my soul.

Weepin' cleanses,
I guess,
too much rot
dried 'round
yo' dreams,
huh?

Peel the skin off, Tula.
Better that way.

Steal one every day.

She borrows a flower

Kitchen
could be
a field,

if we want.
Lots of flowers
danglin' off
they stems,
all colors.

Picnic field.
God's good table.

That's why
you cry:

huh, Tula?

We's sisters,
ain't we?
Even though
we jumped
from different
wombs.

I feel yo' tears
on my cheek,

but I ain't
lonely,
an' I ain't
happy
an' I ain't
in between

So what we
doin' heah
sittin'
eatin'

in the sun
that ain't there?
In the kitchen
that ain't a field?

Where you,
Tula?

Dead.
Buried you
yesterday,
jes' 'fo'
you got
too old

cold
in my bosom:
'member?
My last an'
listenin' friend,

an' I got me
a field

to yield
all the flowers
I wants

all kinds of colors.
no leftovers,

right behind
yo' grave.

Borrowed a woodlily
from you, Tula.

Gave it to myself,

(yo' chair be empty)

for my picnic.

Jenny in Love ॐ

Danced in the evenin'

              while

the supper
burn;

whupped

                   in the morning:

danced again!

Hattie on the Block

Remember me?
I'm the woman you nailed to a tree
after the twilight died.

Carrie, you be still, now,
   don't make no noise.
Mama will protect you
   from all the shoutin' an' screamin'
   an' biddin' that's goin' on
      right now. Hold on. Hold onto Mama.
   Won't be long now,
   they done had they lunch,
   an' somethin' will happen to take
   the fear outta your bones
      an' the sweat off of your eyelids
   an' drain them to the sweet winds
   for the birds to eat. Somethin' will happen:

Happens that I be a slave woman,
maybe that makes me property,
not a human bein' like all
you who come to buy me,
see if I'm sturdy, can hold ground,
can withstand the elements, bear fruit

when the seed is in me, like the Lord's land,
sing for my supper when the seasons come,
give death the mortgage on my bones.

Don't come near me! Stay away!
I'm not buyable yet,
I'm a bit unleavened.

Still, Carrie, be still, child. Don't cry,
   don't let them see you cry, honey,
there's a victory in that. Keep the tears
   inward, outta they sight.
Hold onto my apron, tear it, if you want,
   hold hard while we crush the evil
pushin' its way through that crowd of shoppers
   yellin' before us an' standin' there
mockin' us with money an' all the changers
   in the temple, but they all look good,
   don't they? Nice coats an' trousers,
   bright shoes, sturdy hats. Ever seen
   a finer lookin' peoples than that?

Evil be pretty sometimes, don't it?

Money look good, even if it be for your soul.

Souls cain't be bought.
I won't be of much use to anybody
who buys me without my Carrie here.
I be crippled, needin' crutches: who gonna
pay for them? Or will I have to work
the fields limpin' about with my mind
catchin' butterflies, when I should be
pickin' cotton, 'cause my soul be amputated
when you bought me without my Carrie
for a few dollars cheaper?

No, don't, I beg, you, don't touch me!
Stay back. I cain't leave this block
in holo-cust!

That's it, Carrie, hang tight;
  My, your forehead be hot,
fever comin' on I 'spect, an' your
  mother's fever gone cold
makin' it more dangerous when
  it be exposed to the elements
that gather up 'round her now,
  this early, bright mornin'
spoiled an' festerin' in the mouths
  of all these happy buyers who need
the disease of your Mama's wrath
  so they can recover from their own
dyin'.

Dyin' today if I be sold without my Carrie.
I promise you that.

Look on us before you lay
your money down. What we cost? $2500?

Good price. Buy what you breed.

Masters, Owners, Buyers, Fathers, Sons,
Take vengeance on your dollar!
God help me, I be His maidservant,
I be His witness to this sale of womanflesh
in the twenty-eighth year of my delivery!

Carrie, look! Wipe your eyes, child.
See. They finished the biddin'. Money
be paid. We's together, God heard my

haltin' words through the ears of these
deafened people; you an' me from this strange
pulpit. Look lively, child. We be sold,
but we ain't bought.

Rya's Rainbow

Oh, the war be a mess.
 I nuss the sick
  and wounded
   on both sides.

Make no difference then, I guess.

Dyin' be dyin', blood be blood:
 see it all now,
  should have been on my way
North with them other folk like Judd

told me to do. But No I stayed
 to wrap the bones
  of the dead
   in a piece of cloth,
sometimes my petticoat, and prayed

for they decent burial. Everything be over.
　　But not me
　　　　I weren't over
　　　　　'till the Lawd
called me and the wings of the mighty ghost hover

over those death fields that wound us all
　　livin' as well as dead
　　　　before the last bell toll
　　　　　before the sun give witness
　　　　　　before the land perish
takin' with it them angry moans that fall

from the mouths of all them that hate
　　and live to like it
　　　　even when it splatters them
　　　　　with dusty demons
eatin' through they souls at misery's gate.

One boy, he be a Yankee, looked at me
　　and begged for water.
　　　　I gives it to him
　　　　　but he pass on anyway,
dry at the mouth, dumb eyes that suddenly

stopped. Oh Lawd, deliver me!
　　So's I nuss
　　　　do my best
　　　　　talk a little
　　　　　　whisper the Lawd's name
where it be prayer properly

wash they wounds, carry they peril and feel
　　my children at my bosom
　　　　and know they hunger
　　　　　and the good of my milk
and hear that terrible rainbow that steal

over the cold land after the evenin' rain,
    touchin' me from inside
        girdin' my strength
            passin' the power of life
                from flesh to ground
with all them colors smilin' on the slain.

Juba in Fire!

I don't want
no favors.
Leave me be!
Git on with yo'
buyin' and sellin'
yo' landownin'
and slaveownin'

Yo' widowin'
and mournin'
and misfittin'
yo' weepin' and workin'
and talkin' and forgettin'
yo' whippin' and stealin'
and breakin' and rapin'
and do what you gotta do,
and leave me be!

Git on with yo'
precious work
and take yo' miseries
with you.

I'm content,
can wash and clean
and cook and give suck
with the best of them
(even the worst—
'cause sometimes
they's strong).
Don't mean no harm,
truly, leave me
be!

Got a passion:
my spirit, wigglin'
and wakin' me up
in the cold mornin's
warmin' my belly
like a new child.

I talk to it,
listen to it,
breathe to it,
make it mine
all over again
every day
every slumber
every little whisper
in my bones
when I wash the grunts
out of my William's ear
or taste the honeysuckle
sweet on my Leah's mouth.

She's a good child,
too good for the mistress—
too merciful and soft.
I'm teaching her to fight
even if it means her death.

No child of mine
gonna go to her grave
while she's still talkin'.

Leah saw me that day.
I wasn't ashamed,
nothin' else to do.
Beat the mistress hard—
tore her clothes off,
gave her a good whuppin',
I did, the way they do
my William when he's too
drunk to feel it,
the way they plan to do
my Leah, if she don't
fight back and kick
when she's able.

Cain't let nobody
touch my skin,
my bone, my long
hard heaven risin'
in my jaw.

Cain't let them beat
Juba or touch the singin'
of her soul. Gotta git
her to heaven in one piece,
her madness inside
like her great Spirit,
risin', risin'
makin' jelly of the moon,
givin' fire to night.

Oh! take me Lord!
I'm on fire!
Carry me to the coolin' waters

and put me inside,
I won't sink, I promise,
I'll float.
I won't die, I promise.
I'll just get over
the bridge that'll
take me to the other side,
and take my fire
with me in a brown
gunnysack that cain't
burn or float
that'll rip me apart
with its weight
until I offer it
some of my ashes.

They's good and clean
and Lord! I believe
They sweeter than life.

They threatened to whup me,
but nobody touch my body
nobody touch my soul
nobody touch my spirit,
nobody in this world.

Then they say they sell me
and sell my baby, too,
so then I take the small one
by the feet, head downward,
upside down,

and I say:
kill me, if you want,
kill me dead,
shoot me in the head,

and send me to glory
or to hell,
but I ain't got a child
for you to sell!

No baby of mine
is you gonna sell,
I'll smash its head
here in front of you,
kill it now 'cause
I done give you five
of mine for you to sell.

Now! send me to glory
or to hell with my child
in my teeth: I tell you,
Marster, yo' property's dead,
right, now!

No sale!
No Juba!

Well, they done sold me,
but not my youngest!
they keeps her,
and I'm here to tell it.

Don't want no favors,
but I'll be dyin' soon,
the signs come
and tell me, like spiders,
cain't work much anymore,
don't care, the Spirit's
still alive, though,
reachin' for my eyes,

I watch it heat
and melt: nothin' more
now. Lost my misery
to a blue-jay.

A Slightly Colored Lady

I was birthed in bondage, lived in Virginia,
my Maw was a slave, my Paw a white man.
Guess I'm 'bout ninety years ole,
I guess.

In slavery you had to be good or you'd
make Marster mad and he'd sell you
or beat you or both. If you were
good and happy and knew how to sing a little

you'd be a pleasure to yo' mistress and marster
and they'd keep you well. You'd eat well:
chicken and corn and poke and beef and lamb,
vegetables, fruits, figs, butter and milk.

And you wouldn't hear dem screams
of other slaves who'd be caught and beat
in the night. And you wouldn't hear their souls
goin' to glory.

And you wouldn't know 'till it 'twas too late
'bout Jonah who be sold 'way from his family
and Lilliemae who stood on the auction-block
on one of dem certain days, and get sold away

from her chillun and how she screamed and kicked
'till her nose bleed: you wouldn't know that
'till 'twas too late, and anyways knowin' don't
bring the dogs home, don't make the moon rise quicker.

And I was happy. Dyin' happy. Happier more
the day I married with my white dress trimmed in pink
ribbon, with my Jessie on my arm. He a teacher.
Later he teach me to read. He good man. Never a slave.

I used to be brighter in color than I is now.
Three, four shades whiter, almost as white
as that weddin' gown, 'cause my mother was nearly white

    white as sorrow
    wrapped 'round a cloud:
    white as the wind
    dancin' in a shroud
    white as summer
    white as death
    white as the moon
    risin' in her throat
    white as the words
    tremblin' as she spoke

Yes. Nearly white. Here lately I'm becoming dark
like ginger-cake, and I wonder if the Lord
don't think it's time for me to go 'long
somewhere else where maybe colors be as you let them

and cain't bring no misery.

Lula's Green Scarf

Minerva give it to me
this heah green scarf
wrapped 'round my neck
like a pretty necklace.

Minerva tell me to wear it
only when I'm rightin' myself,
only when somethin' come 'long
that puts me in danger, tries

to gobble me up. That happens
quite a lot nowadays to us
women slaves who take matters
into they own hands too often.

We got no "Matters," Massa keep
tellin' us. We's slaves, not even women,
Massa says, 'cause women's foolish,

step outta they place too often,
don't give the devil his due,
strut 'round like they's precious
power from the Lawd, Himself.

At least that's what Massa say.
Missus don't pay him no 'tention,
jes keep charge of things, like
she always do, winkin' at me

from the corner of any room she find
me in. Don't know how I figure in all this,
I'm a woman and I'm a slave, and one seems
to cancel out the other. But Minerva say no!

They be things to stand up for, Be for,
believe for. What things, I say.
Yo'self, Minerva say. Am I a thing? I say,
Minerva don't answer. She jes' give me a hug.

She sold a year ago to some place
in South Carolina, not too far away
from heah. Massa say she too uppidy
to be any good on the plantation.

He likes his property with fences, he say.

Whenever I feel my uppidy, I wears
the scarf, green and woolly and scratchy
at times, remindin' me of Minerva and how
she left it on the supper table for me,

for everybody to see, after she left.
I puts it in my pocket before Massa
ask any questions, and called out to Minerva

in the night, with my eyes watery:
I got it, Minerva. This heah scarf
be the umbilical cord between you and me,
rough though it be, and the salvation

of the good things you learnt me to take
for myself. Minerva, you a generation behind me
and you give me myself. Lawd give you to me in prayer,
maybe to cease the prayer that have no hindsight.

I thank you, Minerva.

So when Massa sold Minerva,
I wears the scarf.

When Aunt Sarah died,
I wears the scarf.

When Massa beat Missus for bringin'
water to the field hands,
I wears the scarf.

When I hears of Minerva's 'scape
from that plantation in South Carolina,
I wears the scarf.

When I be asked to watch the whuppin'
of 'nother slave,
I wears the scarf.

I keeps it clean and untattered,
puts it under my head at night,
and when the dark be at its brightest,
I reach, and gives it my blessin'.

Lucy Sleeps with Master Muford

He come
in the night,
it be dark,
no moon.

He do some
funny things
to me
(weren't mischief)
then he die
in my arms.

Polly and Platt

All she could do was call my name:
Platt! Platt!

for I had beaten her all I could
'til I could scourge her no more
and then Ephrim, our Master,
finished the job.

Platt! Ah, Platt!

Like a calling to hell, my own,
since I had given her the first wound
but not of my own will: because Ephrim
held the whip over me and forced me into it.

She lay tender

sighing out of her spirit
asking mine for courage,

in a way, forgiving me.

What had she done?
Borrowed soap from her neighbor,
asked Molly, the Black woman
married to her owner, for something
to get clean, because

she had lain with Ephrim
and he would have it no other way.

She needed cleanliness.

And he took her even in the middle
of her punishment:

(Was it that? Was something out there
punishing Polly for her big spirit
that let her sleep with a crippled
monster, and she, with impunity?)

As she lay in tallow-wax to heal
her bleeding back, he opened her wounds
over and over again, and the wax melted
and let out the pus that mingled with
his white flesh that was no longer white,
but smelled of damp mold and what
she knew of burial and death.

She could bring no child from that.

Platt!! Ah, Platt!
I'll go to hell, Platt, she moaned,
and I'll find him there, I will,
hissing and steaming and dripping
sour growls and breaking into me
like a hot lash. Devils don't hiss
as well as he when he plunges into my body,

my soul!
Ah, Platt!

and her spirit left.

Though she's alive, she ain't.
She don't exist no more.

Her body moves through the house
like a phantom and vanishes at sunset
and no one ever knows where she goes,

not even Ephrim.

When next we see her, sometimes before
the rise of the first light

on the hill

she's moving like ash, floating about
in pieces, her head hung like a scarecrow,

and her smile don't jump into your throat
and make you happy,

the way it used to

when she was herself, walking through daisies
giving God His chores.

Aunt Mary with Papers

Ah wants de wind in mah sorrow de las' breathin' of mah
lil' sister holy on mah tongue   She be killed you know
Murdered by Old Princess   mah mistress   who whupped
   huh ta death
jes 'cause she cried lak all babies do   My lil' Lucie-sister
nine months old   An' Old Princess an' me we had it one
   day when ah
was ten year-old an' she tried to beat me wid an old rod
   and ah took me a
handful of rock and threw it ta her eyeball   busted it and
   told her dat
was for beatin' my lil' sister ta death   But oh!   dat be long
   ago too
long ta watch   mah life ain't cold 'nuf for all dat
   sorrow   No lawd!
Had a marster who made me free   gave me papers an'
   bread an' meat
an clothin' an' a trip in a stagecoach ta find mah
   mother   Dat be mah
birthin'   mah genesis   first day   be earth an'
   star   den   wind an' sea
den bird an' lamb   den man and woman   den
   freedom   den Me!   Ah got
de papers right here somewhere in a trunk of mah
   mem'ry   Mary!   you

71

'member de river dere near Natchez an' de big boat slidin' down huh
spine an' de sunlight glistenin' on huh shoulders lak silver   lak
Sunday jewels   An' you 'member de crayfish caught up in de net
an' de hot beans an' yo head so dizzy not even God could keep it
straight!   Yes   Lawd!   Happy times   you know   not even belongin' ta
someone else and bein' paid for, not even bein' somebody's propuhty
can kill de secret joy dat God put in mah bosom when He made me Mary
an' gave me a fine-spun cloak ta wear ta ride on a mule ta take me ta
de Promised Land   for dis is how ah gits ta Texas   on a mule   out of
de murderin of Cain an' Abel   an' lets me down in de House of de Fust
Bone

Liza Lily in Silks

Oh, this is a quiet dress.
   Light. Airy.
   I can take off soft

in it anytime I please
   if only to tease
   Edam. Get him away

from the horror of his hope
   that traps him in that
   house that both of us hate.

I wait.

These silks are so fine:
   one dress after another
   he gives me.

Green, yellow, like the sun,
   white. Next to my skin
   they dance coolly, gently.

Whirlwinds. Touchin's of song
   and sorrow inward, outward,
   and Edam comin'

in the noon, never the night,
   dressin' me in them
   cryin' me in them

takin' hold of my little life
   in them, squeezin',
   laughin' to my

heartbeat, sometimes just long
   talkin': him and me.
   See. Nothin' else.

And her: missus, botherin'
   to come into my room
   at night and watch

me sleep. Makin' sure I'm alone,
   but I don't know which
   one of us is the slave:

her or me. She has to go
   to his bed, he has
   to come to mine. Fine.

He says I give him peace,
   but what does he
   give me?

Got my hope wrapped in a string
   through my hair,
   I don't care

where I wear it. It's mine
   more than him
   more than me.

My hope and me, we sometimes
   are strangers.

He can't give me hope though
   he talk to me about
   marryin': we marryin'!

I can't see that.
   Don't know why,
   but I can't.

Too much *can't* in my life
   but I got
   silk dresses glistenin'

announcin' Liza before she
   comes, causin' eyes to shudder
   misery to melt.

I'm unbound, singin':
   'round, 'round
   in that special day
   my love he come
   to carry me away.

No Jordan drownin' me!

Soon I'll go for a stroll
   in my blue silk dress,
   go into town

and buy myself a plum,
   the blackest from the tree.

Oh, now, here he come!

Jenny in Sleep

Nothin' be as terrible

                 as sleep

nothin'
be as bright, either.

I come and go

          as I please.

Jo Abandoned

I couldn't go with him   Had my children to think of
Had my heart and my worry to think of   He be determined
Wanted to join Moses and go to the Promised Land   I had
other journeys   some 'scapin to do in my own way   Some
perils to face and clobber and catch by the tail before
I die   Things be blurry   Not too much too clear   I loves my
Jack   Didn't want to see him go   Didn't want to live
in his absence   But I'm fastened to my life here Can't
get away   Can't risk the children too much   Things too
temporary   Jack gone now two years   Haven't heard a word
Suppose he be safe and sound in some fried apple kitchen
maybe with a better wife than I be   Maybe not   If I know
him he be whistlin' by a tree thinkin' of his good fortune
and where he be goin' from there   Thinkin' I be a fool woman
not to follow   Thinkin' night be day and day night and never
the two come together Jack can't stretch his mind too
much to twilight or dawn and he never heard of midnight
'till I asked him not to leave me and the children here
by ourselves   That be midnight for Jack   That be an
inbetween he couldn't maneuver but he could feel it
At least I think he could   Though his feelin's be slow
they usually firm and honorable   Just wanted the best
Jack always wanted the best for himself   I didn't fit
too much his strange wantin's and desires   Didn't fit
that at all   Too bad   I weren't much help   He left at

77

midnight   Watched him pull his angry body through the
dark   Stayed awake while his footstep warmed from the
shed   then took me to sleep.   Yes   he be whistlin'
somewhere a pretty good tune and I be listenin' here in
my dark and safety for a footstep that won't ever again
bear my name   Ain't no return   Jack   Ain't no return
The lamp be let too low   Never liked carrying lamps
noways   They only give shadows and yours be too shrunk
Jack for me and the children not to stumble over
But the shadow   be wide a little too and that be too much
for this place to handle   These here folks can't bother
much with fieldhands with wide 'spectations of themselves
Gotta go now   Missus still askin' me questions 'bout
where you go an' how I feel 'bout you leavin'
    abandonin'
me she says   Got another lie ready for her for you Jack
which I make every mornin' like grits and butter
She likes the taste   Whistle to that   Honey

Sidney, Looking for Her Mother . . .

But suh, you've made a mistake. Oh, yes suh! I can't be

    put

on the block no more. I'm free. See. Here be my papers. I

    know I've

got a brand on the back of my neck, as you've noticed, but

    that be from my first

master 'cause I run away too much, but my new master

    gave me my freedom! And

my mistress packed a big basketful of food—more than I

    could eat, enough

for three people!—and gave me money to take the train

    and go to my

freedom and my mother. Oh, my mistress and master be

 good people. Lord

Bless 'em. Now, please let me go 'long. My mother is out

 there somewhere

and you detain me unlawfully. Do you understand the

 papers, suh? Can you

read? No offense, suh. Oh, no! but the train for Austin be

 here any

minute and that be the place where last I heard my mother

 was.

I don't know how strong she be, if all the days of her

 motherhood

be for the mothers of children without mothers, though

 they mothers

be close in they rooms, in they chatters, and in they

 dreams and

playthings, all that motherin' of children, all white and

 fragile,

playin' in the sunlight when the ease of the wind be on

they faces,

and they hungry cheeks, and they fade sometimes in they

playing and need

a kiss for they misery. All that motherin' while mothers sip

and sip tea with they kin and talk about the beauty of the

magnolia or the rose bush

or how expensive they silver be and how much they pay

for they woman slaves

when they be young and child-bearin' and cheap, and

sometimes they mother

a horse with tenderness and affection, brush him daily,

keep him well-fed,

give him a special doctor, and weep when he's ailin', or

mother

they chatters with friends and mother they fears and

memories.

I wonder, suh, I don't know, but I wonder if all that

   motherin' which

my mother makes out of clay, sometimes hasn't muted her,

   made her silent,

you know, invisible. But I must go, please suh! I must find

   her and Austin

is where she was last seen, which means her strength be

   there, her visibility,

movin' throughout the land like a moonbeam, takin' care of

   those other than herself.

She be my mother, suh. Do you recognize the sound, if not

   the word? Don't holler,

suh, please don't holler. I'm sick of hollerin', so sick it

   don't scare me

no more. But your throat sounds raspy and must be sore.

   Hollerin' don't help any.

Oh, now! Do you hear it? The train be comin' and I be a

   passenger. The papers,

suh, may I have them back? They simply tell that I'm free,

can't be put on the

auction block no more. You understand? This man here

standing next to you can

look at them, if you like, if you give them to him, please,

suh, quick the train

be. . . . You understand, now? Oh, thank you, suh, thank

you. I thought you would.

Here be the train. I have one seat and my mother in my

lap, on my arm, in my

belly, on my tongue, through my eyes. All that and more.

She out there.

I know it. Gotta get me a seat. And wonder.

. . . As Her Mother Waits

*The kitchen be dark today, not much light comin' in from de
    windows.*
Maybe it means somethin': Ah jes don't know.

                    We be,
                    Sidney an' me.

Here Lately

They be fifteen
chillun comin' 'long,
Black an' white,
my Marster's an'
mine and dem's
from other slaves.

Ah keeps busy,
don't do nuffin'
but nuss,
sometimes dey be
chillun pullin'

from both sides:
white on one,
Black on ta'other
pullin' away,
keep me busy.

84

Dey's scream
at night an' cry,
only way ah keeps
dem quiet be fo'
ta outscream dem.
Dey gits tired
an', awed,
an' be silent.

Swing low,

Cain't think
too much of my
Sidney
where she be
how she be
if'n she 'member me.

She jes' a 'lil
bitty thing when
ah be sold away
to Marster Aaron
in Opelousas, Louisiana.

Ah 'member huh
bright eyes
an' honey-rich skin
as ah squeezed
huh 'lil hand
'fo ah left
'till it turned red.

She be six-year ole
an' beautiful
with huh high
cheek-bones, long legs
an' huh yaller dress
I made for huh
from pieces of
ole cloth.

Ah 'member dat,
ah 'member dat well
'cause she don't cry,
'ah do, but she don't,
an' ah don't look back
when dey tote me away
in de mule wagon.

Sweet Chariot . . .

But marster
wouldn't let me be
no mid-wife lak
ah wants, he didn't
believe in booklarnin'
for no slave 'cause
bright niggers don't raise
good sugar-cane. Law hep me,
I'se good at wet-nursin',
though, don't need
no papers.

Wid all dat nussin'
of chillun comin' 'long
so fast, it done stunted
mah growth an' dat's why
ah ain't tall an' straight
lak ah used to be, jes'
skin an' humped bones.

Paradise

Mah Sidney!
Lawse' mah
lovely Sidney!

We's willows
in de grass.

Heah in Texas
I'se free
but lonely, achin'
all over, under
de weather most
of de time.
Marster Aaron
gib me mah freedom
when de war came.
He good man.

Married again,
mah fust husband
went mad an' jumped
in de Mississippi
river soon's ah sold
away from him
to Marster Aaron,
neber could stand
affliction of any kind.
Died next day.
He be blessed.
Lawd blessed him
goodly, kindly.

But mah second husband
strong, free man.
Worked hard as a carpenter,
died of yellow fever
one feverish night,
holdin' mah hand
as Marster Aaron did
when he passed on.
Wouldn't die, Marster,
'til ah come back
to Opelousas jes'
to be by his bed.

They be lies heah in de night,
they be ghosts an' mothers wantin'
chillun to kin in de night,
'cause dey's feelin' da fright
dey cain't feel when things be
even an' clean lak lullybyes
hung in de light.

Pick one, Sidney,
de lullybye wont you
to give it a home.

Now, mah big girl, make yo' mother
a tatterin' home in yo' bosom.
It be through yo' wantin' dream
you done hep me undie.

> *Comin' fo' to carry me home . . .*

Well, let me get on:
I'se a paid nuss now
an' lil' Miss Rachel
needs huh breakfast.
She woke up feelin'
better dis mornin'.

She likes peeled fruit and cream.

Lottie in Lullabies

Bluebird, bluebird t'rough yo' window,
Bluebird, bluebird t'rough yo' window,
Bluebird, bluebird t'rough yo' window,
Oh, Johnny, I'm tiahed.

Pitipa needs sleep,
   He be so cast down at night, when I be away
in the fields bringing water to the men laborin', sweatin'
   achin'. Yes. Pitipa be a bit downcast, have to lullaby
him to sleep, give him his lovable music and the feel of
my hips
   under his soft, little feet that curve 'round my waist
like tender vines, an' I dance an old chant, song of
my grandfathers
   and them's before, song of him wrapped to my back
   with soft muslin
head leanin' strong in my bones and ribs, like the comfort
of a good,
   sturdy chair. *Take that little boy, pat 'im on the shoulder,*

take that little boy, pat 'im on the shoulder,
   take that little boy, pat 'im on the shoulder,

Oh, Johnny, I'm tiahed.

89

An' my Pitipa soon begins to fall asleep softly, ever
so quietly,
    gently, no whimperin', 'cept to cry out a little from a
    scary dream,
some great monster he see when the wind done
stop blowin'
    an' all the dark would be puffy an' moist an' movin' into
    his mouth
an' his ears, an' his eyes, an' he know the watery blackness
    that will come one day in the fields when I be old
    and slow,
no back to pillow him, jes' water from my hands an' a
weak pat on the head
    to help him 'long when he picks the cotton and bales
    it in.
Oh, Johnny, I'm tiahed!

Here we go 'round the mulberry bush, the mulberry bush, the
mulberry bush,
    here we go 'round the mulberry bush so early in the morning.
This is the way we sweep our flo', sweep our flo', sweep our flo',
    this is the way we sweep our flo' so early in the morning.

Maybe that be his dream, *'round the mulberry bush, the*
mulberry bush,
    long 'way ahead of time, checkin' out his young
    manhood when it comes
down the road for him to grieve an' chant, *this is the way,*
    but now my Pitipa sleeps an' I dance lightly 'round
    the room,
swayin' from side to side', in fine litanies, *this is the way we*
brush our
    hair, brush our hair, brush our hair, feelin' his body give
    an' bounce,
glad to be his mother, my last-born, glad he be with me in
the evenin' songs,
    glad he be with me in the rain, *this is the way we plant*
    the wheat,

plant the wheat, plant the wheat, this is the way we glad
my voice
    don't shiver an' fall in the stable, glad the song be in my
      throat to
plant the wheat so early in the morning, this is the way we plow
the land

    plow the land, plow the land,
    this is the way we plow the land
    so early in the morning,

an' come out good.

Anne's Hideaway

Last night, bright in the stars,
I saw a moonbeam reach across
the field and ride upon the night
like a jealous lover grittin' his teeth.

I grit my teeth and took me
to my hideaway under the big
old house and lay there with my breasts
bared before the breath of the damp

and holy wind. I washed my hair
in the fresh, new and good ground made
by the mornin' rain, and I heard someone
come, saw the shiny boots movin' up

the flat stairs over me, then someone
else and someone else, all night long,
or was it night? I don't know. One
darkness is just like another, but the

moonbeam stayed and I made love to it
softly, singin' under my tongue, like
the otter I saw one day down by the river,
found my laughin' body speed into a big

hole, empty-like, whirlin' and whirlin'
outside myself, because I was lyin' in
the mud under the big house. There be
screams inside me that wouldn't come out.

No, I weren't afraid, I be happy,
in great deliverance, and the moonbeam
whispered, hot on my cheek: *Anne, you be
pure. Untouched. No one has ever
touched your purity. You be clean.*

*Forget all those happenin's with all those
greedy men, that labored lovemakin' in those soft
beds that never welcomed you, only praised
the rooms of the big house. That weren't real.*

*You be sold to that whenever he needed you
to make a little extra money to keep
his business goin'. That be all. Forget . . .*

Oh, Moonbeam! Be still! You not there!
I saw you die last mornin' and you
never come back. You never rode the sky
like you said you would. I dream all that up.

I don't remember you no more, but you rattle
in my brain too much, you play 'round with my
skinny memory 'til I think there be two persons
pullin' at my muddy soul and you be in the middle

keepin' us apart. Sometimes I'm Me. Sometimes I ain't.

*. . . Forget you ever come here. You ain't here, Anne.
That be a crumpled shadow coolin' itself under
the big house!* I hears the moonbeam grumble.
Then I says to myself: ain't no moonbeam,

that's trash. I'm poor white trash.
Whatever black in me done crawled away
lithe and limpin', gone to earth, wounded, wet,
two by two, under the spiny big house.

Julia, Carrying Water

Well, I carries things,
water in a glass

on my head
sometimes a bucket

and I never spills
a drop,

though I walk through
briars and bristles

up hills and over
stony paths

in rooms brightly dark
with watery movin'

shadows, before my mistress
stumblin' on the stair.

I walks straight into
the mouth of a doorway,

say, Good evenin' all,
water's here, and I never spill

a drop.

Gravity Sews a Seat Cushion

Nearly goin' blind,
lookin' for myself all over
the place,   *the place,*

cain't find all of me, all the
time, just enough to settle down by for a little,
the moment   *the moment,*

when the winter winds blow
over my shoulder and give me
a peek   *a peek,*

at myself. Just too old now
to make sense, but I remembers
slight things   *slight things*

like ghosts hangin' out there
in a tree waitin' for me
to come   *to come,*

and give them body and shape.
Sewin' be my livin', my talent,
I guess,   *I guess,*

makin' things for the mistress: her dresses,
nightgowns, party clothes, even gloves
sometimes,   *sometimes;*

though they's not my best sewin'.
Naw! Before I gets too blind, and
be doleful   *be doleful,*

my best sewin' be my cushions
all decorated with flowers and peaceful
little   *little*

figures, most of the time chillun,
with they tender faces and pink cheeks,
the way   *the way,*

my missus like to see chillun,
'cause she hardly ever look at my sweet Ellen
and strong   *and strong;*

Aaron when they see her in
the doorway in the afternoons watchin' for
somethin'   *somethin'*

or someone to come have tea with her
in her brand new parlor that I done
sewed   *sewed,*

together all by myself. But she liked
my seat cushions, say they soft and pretty and give
respect   *respect*

to her house. I 'member one day, just
before my blindness struck me, I saw my mistress
walkin'   *walkin'*

through that room like she be a queen
of Carolina. She had a tiny waist that the marster
always   *always.*

liked to squeeze his hand 'round
and that day she wore her lovely, silk yellow dress that
I made: *I made:*

she looked like a queen, too. Straight. Even. But I
noticed somethin' then that turned me 'round and 'round,
made me   *made me*

dizzy and dumb through my insides, set my brain afire
and cold burns of pain through my whole body, as Missus
  stooped
over   *over,*

to pick up a doll from the parlor floor
that her little Lotus done dropped. Why, that
tiny   *tiny,*

waist was suddenly invisible and all that be there be
a wide bottom that seemed to stretch at those hips, openin'
  up
wider   *wider*

and wider, slowly stretchin' like the mouth of a cobra,
and a terrible, awful thing happened to me as
I witnessed   *I witnessed*

that strange and mockin' sight. I knew that this be
what brought her chillun into this world, and this be
the genesis   *the genesis*

and larder of the chillun that owned me now and would
  own my chillun
and they father and would for generations tempt the devil
'til   *'til*

he face the moon and forget to howl, and I believed as I
  chilled
and shook that the good book didn't intend for it to be that
  way, that
there be   *there be*

99

mercy out here somewheres and I'se goin' to find it
if it be willin' to look an old seamstress in the face.
Mercy: *mercy:*

So one night when all's asleep, I snuck into that
precious parlor in the dark and sewed tiny briars and
thistles   *thistles*

in missus favorite chair. Next day she come down for
    breakfast, sat, jumped up
bleedin' and screamin'. Then the doctor come, covered her
    back cheeks with powder
and salt   *and salt,*

like he did me after I'se beat, and we both suffered
    together,
even cried on each other's shoulders 'cause of the pain, but
my tears   *my tears*

be no help, no help at all, and after that she shun me.
But the marster never touched her much again, 'cause she
complained,   *complained,*

couldn't lay on her back, and me, all that sewin' all them
    years
in the cold and dark and that final labor blistered my
    troublin' eyes,
caused me   *caused me*

to be no good at sewin' no more. After that they sold me
    and I'se
where I is now, sweepin' floors, washin' pots and pans,
    haven't seen
a needle   *a needle*

in fifteen years and haven't seen the devil
hangin' out there beyond the window waitin' in a tree,
waitin'   *waitin'*

for my body, either. My sight's gone home. In broad
    daylight
it took off like a swallow and flew to higher ground. That
where   *where*

the light comes in peaceful flagons sprinklin'
itself over me like a rainshower, that where
my soul be.   *my soul be.*

Harriet in Mid-Air

Tubman, the Lady

Lately, I sees dark stains before my
eyes, an' I'm ready to go.

Lately, I hears chants in the eaves
of my dreams an' I'm ready,
I'm ready to go.

Lately, I needs to pronounce
my name in a hundred ways,
in faces, not marster's fields,
in cities an' towns an' places
that bear my footprint,
not my tired an' achin body.

an' I'm ready to go!

An' deep river, my home
is over Jordon in the last land
of the Almighty where life be
my witness at the fallin' day

an' I'm ready to go once,
twice, three times *sold!* three times seven
seven times one thousand *gone!* out into
my first baptism

where the lions go

where the last night flickers
where I put my breath to the lantern
an' make it burn.

So, John, goodbye an' how y'do,
your Harriet will be waitin' for you,
if you come,
if you come.

Stand by the willow tree,
where first you honeyed me,
an' I'll come for you,
I'll come for you.

I know you be frightened,
an' I be, too,
but I'll come for you,
just for you.

Can't make it together,
no way, no how,
John Tubman, my husband,

you be late with courage,
you be unable to move,
you be my love an bendin' life.

Let me know when you're ready,
an' I'll come for you
as you came for me,
under the fragile willow tree.

Sing, oh sing, Harriet!
You be between here and now
the last hours of the Lord's eye
watchin' you now as you go.

The labor be truly conceived,
mine at last!

Miss Maggie's Little Room

I saw my mother in a dream last night.
She was quite young! About fifteen,
I would guess, and lovely and bright
through her deep brown skin. How strange an apparition!
I could not touch her, or tell her that I loved her
and missed her. In fact she was sitting on a stool
in a glass room made of crystal; some other slave folk
were around her, talking in whispers, but I could not hear
or recognize them, and they appeared to shun me, not harshly
or meanly, but gently with the tremors of compassion.

I called, Mama, come here. Let me hold you!
For I could not seem to move toward her.
But she did not answer. Oh, how I felt
her presence in that room, but I knew that she did not
feel mine, perhaps not as strongly. Then she vanished.
What happened next still stuns my heart! The slave folk
melted into the glass. They left no footprints, but their
visages suddenly became the glass that shaped the room
and the room itself was suddenly empty; only the crystal
visages in shades and shadows, distortions, some clear,
some not, remained. I saw myself reach for the shadows,
hoping one of them would be Mama, but she was gone,
young and sweet. Truly.

She left only her presence for me to embrace.
I think she tried to speak before
she vanished, though she never looked at me;
yet, I felt her voice stride through my lungs
softly, and I wanted her first fifteen years,
all of them, for my own. She in me, over and over again,
now and forever, Amen.

Then I awoke, remembering the glass room,
the shards of blues and greens and yellows
reflecting into that room. In my head I placed
within the room children to be taught, instructed,
cared for. I tried not to remember the dream,
as it was somewhat painful. I put into the room
Sadie's child, Henry, who seems to know how to add
numbers naturally; and little Tessie, who has chosen
not to speak to anyone; and William, who rides horses
well when Mr. Pembroke lets him; and Millie, the flirt!
who loves words; Jenny, the poet, and Peter, who draws
nicely; Abraham, who is fascinated by maps, and oh,
so many others, rounding themselves in the spaces these
people allow them to have, like leavings from Sunday's
dinner, they singing for their supper, their talents
enemies of their owners, their beholders unable to walk
in the sun without getting bloated, while these little ones
catch the life of their dreams in their eyes.

Yes, somehow the night of that vision, for I know now
it was not a dream, the glass room awakened me.
It has been awakening me ever since, with a chill
that leaves my fingerprints on its doors. The room
is unbreakable. I know that. And my mother kisses
its doors and leaves no breathprint, only whispers
of her apocalypse that lean against the ceilings of
my memory. I know that, too.

I speak these things to no one, for nobody remembers my mother who died alone in the coldness of a farm in Ohio. She was sold away from this plantation some twenty years ago, when I was just fifteen. And no one that I have encountered here believes in glass rooms.

Jenny in Tears

What a salty world
                    this be,
hot an' wet,
        the river runnin' down my throat,
lungs achin'
        all day through.

Misery won't last long, Jenny,
        Mamas come an' go,
Mine go sellin' good.
        Quick. Head up.
Leave your salty water
        in the well, girl,
for a dusty day!

Cora Sue's Options

War be finished. Prayers be finished, too.
   All I need to do is to make a decision:
   stay or go. All I need to know is which
   to do, an' take my way from there.

God done come an' answered Cora Sue's prayers:
   Free me, Lord, from this abomination.
   Dressed up my spirit for Him one fine evenin',
   took myself to the prayerfolk dancin'
   in the churchyard, and joined me to
   their singin' celebration.

It all be over now. No more slaves. We be
   workers now. Stay on the plantation,
   if you want an' work for your keep
   or travel on out of this misery;
   but each way holds perils, an' I ain't
   used to such peril-choosin'. No suh.

I'm seventy year old now, an' I looks for guidance.
   Looks to the Good Lord who give me, Cora Sue Apton,
   for the first awful time such shoutin' come's
   an' go's, takin's an' leavin's; looks to the Lord
   in winesome wonder. But God be dancin', too.

Tildy's Prayer

Saw an angel
on the hill
last night,
all naked and red
in the skin,
'cept his boots,
though he be white.

Smelled funny,
talked funny, too.
Name was Rudy,
Called me Lucretia,
told me God
wanted to see me,
danced, and caught
my arm.

I laughed
and screamed,
and hollered, spat
in his eye,
had a fit,
called on the Lord,

wretched myself
from that specter's
hold and harm.

Run away backwards.

He disappeared.

Althea from Prison

> *Stone walls do not a prison make,*
> *nor iron bars a cage.*
> —Richard Lovelace,
> *"To Althea from Prison"*

Can't bear no children,
I be barren, captive.

Us slaves all be captive
in this high and mighty land.

No use pretendin',
Can't bear no children.

My body done told me so,
and all them children
I been waitin' for
all these lingerin' years
done told me, too.

They gone somewhere else.
Won't come to me,
not even for a visit.

Captive folk ain't in they blood.

112

Sometimes I see them
disappearin' over the horizon
in they blues and pinks and short shawls,

won't come near me.

Goodbye, y'all.
Come by here one day
before the fear starts
in my bosom, if you got
the inclination,
and birth me clean,
untethered, and comely.

Emma in Deafness

Ain't heard nothin' in years.

There be dreams, too many of them,
too awful of them, too teary and peppery.
I takes the bad ones first,
then the good, gives me a balance,
helps me to remember what I cain't
when I sees folks movin' their mouths
all over me 'till I sneaks out of myself
and leaves my shadow for them to talk to.

The good dreams be safe and honest and I don't
mind takin' them to bed with me instead of my
Joshua, who is long gone, sold to some other
plantation. Wonder if he remembers me?
Wonder if he takes my murmerin' to bed with him
still? He used to. Call me Easy Girl
(I can read signs) 'cause I so easy to be with,
so easy to talk to. Cain't talk back. He knowed
that all along, never cruel about it, just give
me honey to lick and call me 'nother name,
Sweet Tongue, 'cause he knowed I had one.
Always licked the honey from his hard, brown hand.

Miss my Joshua.

Miss myself sometimes, though I make me up
in sweet ginger mornin's that laugh back
at me when folks give me orders that don't
make sense. Don't make sense to sneak 'round
and watch Liza Lily make love to Massa
like she be his wife. Don't make sense
to know he love her back and give her silks
and fine shoes while Missus 'spect me
to give her signs that things be different.
Don't make sense to know too much anyway,

or see too much
or moan too much
or even smile too much.

Moon don't make sense
when it be out there
botherin' me with its spells
and whispers.

Yes, I hears the whispers
all the time,

and my deafness teases me on my tongue,
gives me sounds larger than my ears,
takes all the nothin's away, and the dumbness
speaks and I hears its sweet cry: I knows much
that ain't ever goin' to know me better.
I sees lips movin' and their sounds run 'round me
like a great shower cleansin' me in a natural way,
keepin' me busy. I make up my own commands:
Emma, be happy, Emma, give praise, Emma, sing,

115

Emma, cuss the devil, and I make my own complaints,
too, while all those faces, rubbery and pasty,
follow me 'round all day long.

But I be still.
No sense murderin' what I ain't heard.

Aunt Sarah, Stealing

I takes de white chillun to church sometime, but dey
couldn't larn me to sing no songs 'cause I didn't
have no spirit.

—Sarah Ashley, ex-slave

Us never got 'nuf to eat,
never.

Saw mah chillun hungry,
cryin' in de night,

ax de Lawd to show me
de way, some kinda hope,

some food fo' mah table,
fo' mah sons an' daughters,

jes' dat, nothin' else;
every human needs to feed

demselves to live an' we
had to live, ya know (tho'

sometime I couldn't tell why)
couldn't starve together,

No, suh! So I keeps stealin',
had to, not 'nuff to go 'round

an' de fields be hot an' heavy
an' us be hungry: plain as dat.

Us bring in three hundred pound
a' cotton a day, we's be beat,

so we's need to be strong, ya know,
we needs our strength for da sun

an' da whip an' da salt an' cayenne
pepper we get into da wound.

Oh, dey's be terrible times,
need somepin' better.

Us hides d'food, den us eats
'cause our strength keeps us holy,

'gives us dis dey our daily breads,
de Lawd's prayer says and if'n

de Lawd not go hungry, why should us?
He make it known dat food His property,

not slaves, dat He be Massa, not Mose
Davis who buy an' sell an' sell an' buy

'til he drop dead. One day I stole
a chicken, nex' a pig, woulda taken

a cow if'n I had de body big 'nuff,
like Jessie who tried it one day,

got caught an' trotted on; he lame
now, cain't even tote an empty bucket.

Yes, Lawd, us stole 'til mah spirit
sank under de weight an' broke,

brought it home wid me one day
in a basket, warn't no cotton dere

jes me too soft to blow away,
sometimes couldn't lift my haid,

not 'cause I'se be guilty or sinful
but 'cause de dey be long, go on

fo'ever in mah bosom whar mah
chillun's milk oughta be.

Missus she think I'm sick wid
some disease. She right: mah spirit

sold an' bought. Feverish. Shiverin'!
Lonesome. Need doctorin'. Need safety.

Vera in Trouble

Might as well face it.
Go down the stairs,
smile a little,
do a bugger dance,
act as if nothin' happened,
indulge myself secretly,
welcomin' Vera as a good person.

Watched my Solomon
do a buck n' wing one day
just to stop them
cuttin' off his forefinger
because he tried to learn
to write. They all laughed
so much they forgot his hungry
fingers, only remembered his
feastin' legs.

I'm too brand new to be whipped
an' salted down like a slaughtered
pig, it be too painful to show them
the festerin' of my real wounds,
though they be drippin' all over
the place half the time.
They never see me wipe up the slop.

Might as well face it,
buggerdancin' 'round the stairs,
head back, hips shakin', dress
raised just enough for my ankles
to balance me out prettily, songs
laughin' up at the ceilin', eyes
crawlin' all over their breakin' faces.

They like my chilly chants,
call them nigger music,
then they grabs their hants
outta their stomachs,
an' go chatterin' to dinner.

They forget all about me.
That be good forgettin'.

Sadie Snuffs a Candle

It be the last time I'm snuffin' candles in cold dark
    halls, nobody there but me
        waitin' to be called on
            and do errands.

Now, I'm twenty.
Tomorrow I go to my freedom.

My mistress and me go together.
She leaves a terrible house.
I leaves a dead one.

Her husband decayin' while he still alive,
dyin' in her body while he heats and sweats.

My husband a thief, jackassin' 'round, 'till he be shot
    with a chicken under his coat.

Nonny and me.
We escape together, the two of us:

She say she a slave, too,
not all slaves black and poor,
and she wants her freedom.

I gives it to her
with my spirit movin'
in her shoes.

She gives it back, though
between us it be
a little tattered.

Nonny and me: we each other's age. I her servant,
    she, mine. Good person.

Tonight be the final one.
She sit at the head of the table
for the last time.

Then.

I snuff out with my fingertips
the big lonesome candle
in the wide, broodin' hall.

We now be shadows
still and apart
me and the candle.

I leaves first, then missus leave behind me.
    We travel
            Goodbye, dear Sadie!
                    different ways.

I smell the candle's taper
from the open doorway,
smoke shadows in a rich, black light:

the end of the burnin'.

Hey, Nonny! Go!